Contents

Publisher: Independent Publishing Network
Published 2018
ISBN 978-1-78926-758-7
Author: Sue Walton
www.multipom.com

Introduction

The Multipom is a fun and exciting way to make up to 20 identical pompoms at a time. It's a much quicker and easier way of making pompoms than has previously been possible, which in turn opens up a whole new world of pompom projects.

All sizes, from tiny 1cm diameter up to 12cm diameter pompoms can be made on a Multipom, making it very versatile for many creative projects. Any yarn can be used so it's great fun experimenting with colours and textures whilst creating lots of unique pompoms. This makes it easy to coordinate any colour scheme or project and is a great way to reduce waste by using up oddments of yarns leftover from previous projects.

Each step-by-step project has been tailored for those with basic creative skills, equipment and yarns which are readily available. There are projects to help children learn and practise basic skills, enabling them to create fun, decorative and importantly achievable items. For those who are more experienced, there's room to add their own creative flair and build on the projects shown.

Begin by learning how the Multipom works! Follow the instructions which come with your Multipom pompom maker. Practise making the different sizes shown and try using a variety of yarns. These instructions will form the basis of everything in this book.

A pair of strong sharp scissors and a large-eyed needle is all that is required to make and attach the pompoms although a basic sewing kit and a sewing machine may be useful too. If any other materials are required, this is stated within the individual projects.

Take a look at the website www.multipom.com and follow Multipom on social media, where there's lots more ideas to inspire you.

Get pompomming today the Multipom way!

Materials & types of yarn

Experiment with anything that can be wrapped around your Multipom frame
to create pompoms in all colours, textures and density.

1. The best yarn to begin with is double knitting acrylic. It comes in every colour imaginable, is easy and relatively cheap to buy and makes lovely dense pompoms.
A 100g ball will make over 100 pompoms, each approximately 2cm diameter.

2. Cotton perle, which comes in an array of colours and is sold for crocheting, is a very useful yarn. Not only does it make gorgeous tiny pompoms but as it's very strong, it's useful for tying when using a thicker yarn to make the pompoms. Once made, these pompoms benefit from wetting (see instruction leaflet) to make them rounded and extra fluffy.

3. Multicoloured and rainbow yarn makes beautiful pompoms and can be purchased in many colour combinations.

4. Strips of fabric, either cut or torn, make unusual pompoms. A fine and soft fabric works best. These pompoms could be made from remnants or leftover fabric, to co-ordinate with a project.
Use a strong but thin yarn to tie them, such as perle or embroidery cotton.

5. Fluffy yarn such as mohair makes similarly fluffy pompoms. Brush gently with a teasel brush to raise the pile even further.

6. Pompoms made with 100% wool (here we've used tapestry wool) can be felted after making. Immerse them in very hot water, squeeze most of the moisture out of them and roll up in a towel until they are just damp. Fluff them as normal and dry. They become dense and firm and are more hardwearing compared to unfelted ones.

7. Natural fibre pompoms can be dyed. Make the pompoms and immerse in water to ensure they are completely saturated. They can be dyed one colour or randomly to give a tonal effect. These are made with 100% cotton and dyed using procion dyes.

8. It's fun to experiment with novelty yarns. Hairy yarns always shed fibres when the pompoms are cut or trimmed so be sure to cut them over a bin!

Multicoloured pompoms

Any combination of colours and thickness of yarn can be wrapped together, making it a great way to use up those small oddments of yarn in your stash. This is a really fun and exciting way to create unique pompoms.

1. A variety of different coloured yarns can be combined to make pompoms where the colours are in blocks. In this example, pink was wrapped first, then turquoise on one side and yellow on the other side. The bundle was tied and cut as normal to reveal almost identical multicoloured pompoms.

2. To make speckled pompoms, wrap the frame with any number of colours of yarn at the same time. Any type and thickness can be used too and it's great fun to incorporate a really unusual yarn, like a sparkly one, into the wrapping.

Trimming & fluffing

Get creative and trim your pompoms into any shape or style.

1. Make the pompoms slightly bigger than the finished required size. Using sharp scissors, trim to shape. Don't be afraid to trim them quite a lot, as this will make them more dense.

2. The pompoms can be wetted to make them extra fluffy. Rub in the palm of your hand whilst damp. Alternatively, very gently fluff them with a teasel brush.

Attaching the pompoms

Using the pompoms' ties to attach them, makes them very secure.
We never use glue!

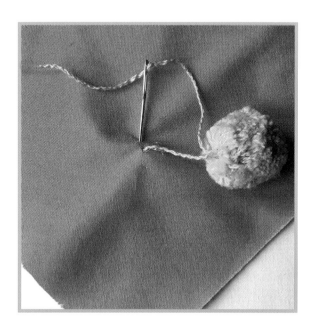

1. When making pompoms ensure the yarn used to tie them is appropriate for your project. If using a thick yarn or making tiny pompoms, use a strong but thinner yarn to tie them. A cotton perle or a stranded embroidery cotton is ideal and are available in a wide range of colours to match the pompoms.

2. Use a large eyed sharp needle to attach them. A chenille needle, size 18 or larger, is ideal. This will pass through fabrics without damaging them.

3. To attach the pompoms, thread the needle with one of the ties and pass through to the back of whatever you're attaching it to. Repeat with the other tie, a short distance away from the first. Tie the ends in a double knot on the back to secure.

4. The ends can be trimmed shorter to neaten, which is all that is necessary if the back of your project is not visible. If it is important that the ends of the ties are not visible, they can be passed carefully back through into the pompom, using the needle, and trimmed off within the threads.

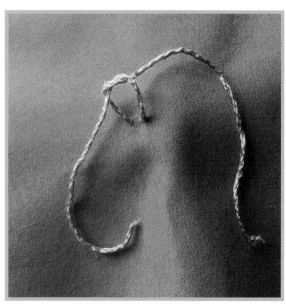

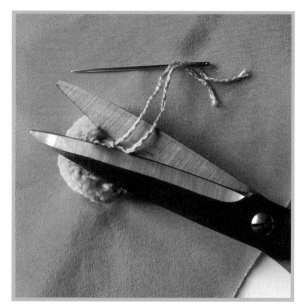

Adding beads & beadcaps

Make your project look extra special by combining beads with pompoms.
Not only do the beads give the pompoms weight but create lovely contrasts in texture.

1. Any beads can be used as long as you're able to thread the tie of the pompom through the hole. Bead caps can be purchased in all shapes and sizes, plain and decorative, but sometimes lots can be found in ready made necklaces and bracelets. Take a look through your old jewellery with the possiblity of upcycling.

2. To ensure the ties will pass through the hole of the beads and bead caps, make the pompoms using a thin but strong matching thread to tie them, such as a perle or embroidery cotton. Pass the ties through the holes in any combination of pompoms and beads of your choice - just let your imagination run wild!

3. Leave the ties long until you have finished attaching them. Pass each tie, separately through to the back of whatever you're attaching it to, a short distance apart, and tie them in a double knot at the back, to secure. Neaten as appropriate.

Tassels

In addition to making pompoms you can use the Multipom frame to make tassels.

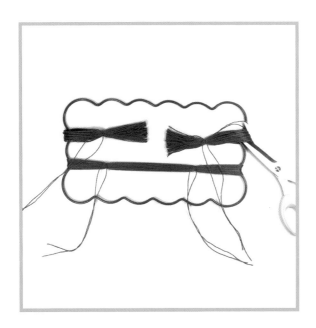

1. Wrap the yarn around the frame fewer times than if making pompoms, as it will be folded over, so doubling the thickness. Tassels work well with a silky yarn, such as viscose, crochet cotton, crepe or perle, but any yarn can be used to suit the style of tassel. Here we're making 4 tassels at a time, each 6cm long by wrapping the frame lengthways using both indentations. Position the ties 12cm apart and 6cm from either end of the frame.

2. Cut the bundle in the centre of the 2 ties; then cut the tassels off the frame at both ends. The ties will be used to suspend or attach the tassels.

3. Keeping the tie at the top, fold the bundle in half and using another tying thread wrap this around the tassel 2 or 3 times approximately 1cm from the top. Pull the tie tight, secure with a knot and pass both the ends into the tassel to hide.

4. Trim the ends of the tassels to neaten.

TIP:
Elaborate tassels can be made by adding beads or pompoms to the ties, stitching the heads or adding cords to suspend them (see page 11)

Twisted cords

Make decorative twisted cords to coordinate with your projects and your pompoms.

To make a single coloured cord:

1. Cut a length of yarn 6 times the length of finished cord required. Tie the two ends together to make a long loop.

2. Secure one end of the loop to a fixed point and put a pencil in the other end. Alternatively enlist the help of a friend and each put a pencil in the loops.

3. Keeping the threads taught, twist the pencil clockwise until tightly twisted.

4. Keeping the tension between the ends, fold the cord in half and allow the threads to twist together from the centre.

To make a two-coloured cord:

1. Cut 2 different coloured yarns, each 3 times the required finished length of cord.

2. Tie both yarns together, making one long loop, but keep the knots together in the middle, so each colour is at opposite ends. Follow the previous instructions, folding in half at the knots.

TIP:
Incorporate additional yarns such as a sparkly lame, a different colour or thickness.

Pompom flowers

Little pompom 'flowers' can be made with a Multipom, by cutting unevenly.

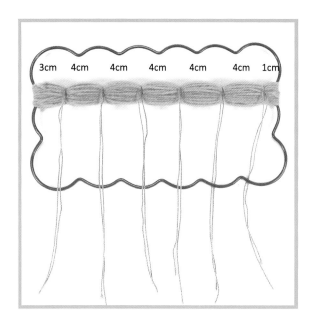

3cm 4cm 4cm 4cm 4cm 4cm 1cm

1. Wrap the frame lengthways 50 times using double knitting yarn.

2. Position 6 ties as follows:
- 3cm from one end.
- 1 cm from the other end.
- the other four, each 4cm apart.

3. Cut the bundle as shown, ie. 1cm from each tie so each pompom has a short side and a long side.

4. When flattened each will make a flower shape.

TIP:
A smaller contrasting coloured pompom could be attached to the back of the flower.

Crochet edging

This very adaptable and simple to make scalloped crochet edging,
with added pompoms, can be applied to a multiple of projects.

MATERIALS: for a 50cm length of edging:
- 15g 4ply cotton yarn plus extra for the pompoms.
- a 3mm crochet hook.
- beads (optional).

TENSION:
16sts to measure 10cm

CROCHET EDGING PATTERN:

Row 1. Determine the length of edging required. For
every 2.5cm required, work 4ch, the total number of
stitches being divisible by 4. ie. for 50cm, make 80ch

Rows 2-4. 1ch, 1dc into 2nd ch from hook to end.
Repeat this row twice more to make 3 rows of dc.

Row 5. 4ch, ss into 4th ch from hook, to end

Row 6. 6tr onto each 4ch loop, ss into ss of previous
row, to end. This will form the scallops. Fasten off.

POMPOMS: using 4ply cotton yarn
Make 1 pompom for each scallop of the edging.
Use the same colour yarn as the crochet edging for the
ties of the pompoms, to ensure it will match when
attaching them.
- Make 12 pompoms each 2cm diameter by wrapping
the yarn lengthways 40 times and tie 12 times.
- Make 16 pompoms, each 1.5cm diameter, by wrapping
the yarn lengthways 25 times and tying 16 times.
- Repeat as many times as necessary.
- Wet the pompoms following the instructions, to make
them extra fluffy.
- Using the ties, attach the pompoms to either the
top of the edging, the bottom of the scallop or both,
adding a bead first if required.

Garland

A quick to make garland for any occasion.

MATERIALS for a 2m long garland:
- Approximately 120g chunky acrylic yarn in colours of your choice.
- Thin but strong yarn for the ties.
- 2.5m of cord (you could make your own - see page 11) or a thin ribbon.
- A chenille needle (a large eyed sharp needle) size 18 or larger, to take the cord.

1. Make 20 pompoms each 5cm diameter. Wrap the frame lengthways 35 times and tie 5 times. Repeat four times in colours of your choice.

2. Tie a loop at the end of the cord for hanging.

3. Make a knot approximately 5cm along the cord (or ribbon if using). Thread the needle with the cord and carefully pass this through the centre of the first pompom, ensuring it passes through the central tied and secured part of the pompom. Tie another knot close into this pompom to stop it sliding along the cord. Repeat at 5cm intervals along the cord until all the pompoms are attached and knotted to secure.

4. If possible, pass the pompoms' ties back into the pompom, through the cord (or ribbon) and trim them short so they are hidden within the pompoms. This will further prevent them sliding along the cord.

5. Make another loop at the end of the cord for hanging.

ALTERNATIVES:
- Beads could be threaded on to the cord, alternating with the pompoms.
- Cut lengths of drinking straws to use as spacers (see instructions for the door curtain on page 38)
- Mix different sizes of pompoms.

Embellished cushion

A perfect addition to any cushion cover.
Attach coordinating pompoms around the edges to give it that finishing touch.

MATERIALS:
- A cushion of your choice. This could be a ready-made bought one, or one you've made yourself.
- Yarn for the pompoms, which co-ordinates with the fabric of the cushion or your colour scheme.
- A strong but thin thread to tie the pompoms.

1. Make enough pompoms in the size and colour of your choice to edge your cushion. Here we've used a 2ply wool and made 48 pompoms, each approximately 2cm diameter by wrapping the frame 100 times and tying 12 times. Repeat this 4 times to make 48 pompoms.

2. Attach the pompoms, one at a time, evenly around the cushion. To do this, use a chenille needle and pass each tie, in opposite directions, through the seam of the cushion, close to the edge. Tie the ends in a double knot, pass them back into the pompom and cut off. This will ensure the pompoms are attached securely.

3. Either pompom all 4 edges or just 2 sides.

Natural blanket throw

Upcycle a blanket by attaching lots of tiny pompoms all over it
to create an eyecatching throw.

MATERIALS:
- Wool blanket 1.60 x 2m
- 200g craft cotton.
- Cotton perle or a similar strong thread to tie the pompoms.

1. Using 2 rulers/tape measures, mark the blanket at regular intervals using a fabric marker or pencil.
We have measured in 15cm squares. These marks will be covered with a pompom.

2. Make enough pompoms to cover each mark on the blanket. We needed 108 (9 across the blanket and 12 lengthways). Using the craft cotton, wrap the frame lengthways 15 times and tie, using the cotton perle, 16 times. Repeat this 7 times to make 112 pompoms.

3. Attach the pompoms by passing each tie through to the back of the blanket, a short distance apart, covering the marks, and tie in a double knot. The ties can be trimmed to leave short ends on the back or pass them back through into the pompom and cut off.

4. If desired, make larger pompoms to attach to the edges of the blanket. We have attached 10 to 2 sides of the throw. These can be any size of your choice, but ours are approximately 4.5cm diameter. and made by wrapping the frame lengthways 140 times and tying 5 times. Repeat this 4 times to make 20 pompoms.

ALTERNATIVES:
- Machine stitch straight lines horizontally and diagonally, joining the dots, and attach the pompoms to the blanket at the point where each line of stitching crosses.
- Place 2 fleeces together and quilt with pompoms through both layers.

Pompom edged lampshade

Transform a plain lampshade into one which is unique and will coordinate with your decor.

MATERIALS:
- A plain lampshade. This one is 15cm tall and 65cm diameter around the bottom edge.
- 25g coloured yarn for the pompoms (we've used double knitting) and a thinner but strong yarn to tie them.
- Approximately 20 coordinating beads with fairly large holes. Glass beads hang well and give the pompoms weight.
- Ribbon or tape to coordinate; long enough to go around the top and bottom of the lampshade.

1. Make the pompoms. If using double knitting yarn:
- For the smaller 1.5cm pompoms around the top of the shade, wrap the frame lengthways 28 times and tie 14 times.
- For the larger 2.5cm pompoms around the bottom edge of the shade, wrap the frame 45 times and tie 10 times, repeating this twice, to make 20 pompoms.

2. Measure around the top of the lampshade and cut the ribbon slightly longer than required. Measure and mark the centre back of the ribbon at regular intervals with a pencil to ensure the pompoms are evenly spaced. Following the marks, attach the pompoms to the ribbon by passing each tie through to the back, a short distance apart. Tie in a double knot on the back. The ends can be cut short or passed back through into the pompom and trimmed off. Continue along the ribbon until all the pompoms have been attached.

3. Make the lower braid of the lampshade by passing the ties of the pompom through a bead, before attaching to the lower edge of the ribbon and tying on the back. The ends can be passed back through the bead and the pompom and trimmed, or cut short on the back of the ribbon.

4. If the lampshade is fabric, the braids can be stitched into place, otherwise they can be attached with adhesive.

ALTERNATIVES:
- Upcycle an old lampshade. If it's made of fabric and a pale tone, the colour can be changed by painting it with silk paint or watered down emulsion paint (leftover from your walls). Dampen the lampshade first, before applying the paint.
- Braids like these can be used to edge a pelmet, blind or curtains.

Suffolk puff cushion cover

Create this gorgeous textured cushion cover using scraps of coloured fabrics topped with little pompoms.

MATERIALS:
- A ready-made 40cm diameter cushion with a plain fabric cover, or make your own.
- Soft fabrics which gather easily; enough to cut 60 x 12cm diameter circles (We've used a polyester lining fabric)
- 60 pompoms, each 2cm diameter, made in a yarn and coordinating colour of your choice.

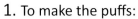

1. To make the puffs:

Cut a pattern out of paper approximately 12cm diameter. You could draw around a plate to do this. Pin the pattern to the fabric and cut out 60 circles in colours of your choice. Using a strong thread and a running stitch, turn in the edges of each circle by 0.5cm. Pull tightly to gather up and fasten off securely to make a puff.

2. Repeat with a variety of coordinating fabrics until you have 60 little puffs waiting for their pompom centres.

3. Starting from the outside edge of the cushion cover, attach the puffs evenly, covering the whole area, ending in the centre. To do this pass the ties of each pompom through the centre of the puff, into the fabric of the cushion cover, and secure on the back with a double knot. By working from the outside edge towards the centre, the cushion cover will remain perfectly round.

Crochet cot blanket

Follow our instructions for crocheting this beautiful cot blanket, finished with gorgeous soft pompoms. All you need to know are 3 simple crochet stitches.

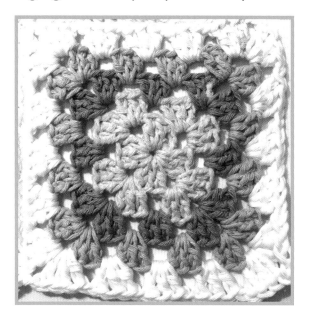

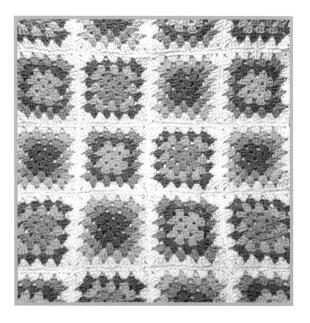

MATERIALS:
- Double knitting yarn. We have used a rustic silk yarn in 4 colours: 50g each of blue, turquoise and lime and 150g of white. Knitting cotton could be substituted.
- Size 7 (4.5mm) crochet hook

1. To make a square
- Work 4 ch. Join with a ss to 1st ch to form a circle.
- 1st round- 3ch, 2tr into circle, 2ch, *3tr into circle, 2ch, repeat from * three more times. Join with a ss into 3rd of first 3ch. This forms 4 clusters.
- 2nd round- 3ch, 2tr, into corner space, *1ch, 3tr into next space, 2ch (to form corner), 3tr into same space, repeat from * three more times. Join with a ss into 3rd of first 3ch.
- 3rd round - Join a new colour. Repeat step 3 noting that the single chain separates the clusters along a row and the 2 chains form the corners.
- Continue working round two more times changing the colour each time. End with the colour you wish to be the linking one.

2. Make 20 squares. Here we have arranged the colours so they repeat and alternate evenly. Before making and joining, arrange the pattern to ensure you have the right colour combinations.

3. With right sides together and using a slip stitch, join the squares together to make rows. Then join the rows together.

4. Edge the blanket with 1 row of dc. Fasten off.

5. Add a pompom to the centre of each square in the colour of the outside round of that particular square. Make the pompoms by wrapping each colour of yarn lengthways 65 times and tying 8 times. Wet the pompoms following the instructions to make them extra fluffy, rounded and dense. Trim them and attach securely to the centre of each square. Pass the ends back through the pompom and cut off to neaten.

ALTERNATIVE:
- Any number of squares could be worked to make a large sized bed blanket.

Pompom quilted bedcover

Keep warm on those chilly nights by throwing this eye-catching quilt over your bed.
It's simple to make using a single duvet, a duvet cover and tie quilted with pompoms.

MATERIALS:
- A single duvet.
- A single duvet cover. Choose a design which would be complimented by adding pompoms.
- Pompoms in colours and sizes of your choice to coordinate with the fabric of the duvet cover.
- A strong thread to tie the pompoms and suitable for quilting with.

1. The duvet needs to fit snugly into the cover and so the cover may need to be altered to fit. Measure the duvet. Turn the cover inside out, and re-stitch one side and the bottom edge so it tightly fits the duvet. Leave an opening at the bottom wide enough to insert the duvet. Trim the excess fabric from the seams, discarding the bottom fastenings.

2. Place the duvet back into the cover and use some long quilting pins to hold it in place at intervals across the whole quilt. Pin and slip-stitch the bottom edge together to close the seam.

3. Make pompoms in the size and colour to suit your fabric. Use a strong but thin matching thread for the ties, as these will be used for quilting. Using a long sharp needle, pass each tie a short distance away from each other, through all layers of the quilt and tie securely in a knot on the back. The threads can be trimmed and left as a feature or passed back through the quilt into the pompom and cut off.

TIPS:
- Instead of using a duvet cover, any fabric could be used for the top and backing of the quilt.
- Use a plain fabric for the backing to make a feature of the ties.
- The edge of the quilt could be piped with either a matching or contrasting fabric.
- This method of quilting could also be applied to a cushion.

Bunting

This pretty lined bunting, with a pompom on each flag, will enhance any room.

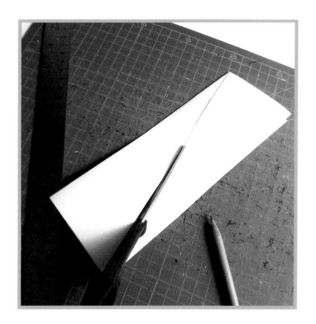

MATERIALS:
- 1/4 mtr of 115cm wide fabric for **each** side (front and backing) of the bunting. This will make 12 lined flags each 20cm long.
- 3 mtrs of tape or fabric, 25mm finished width, to suspend the flags.
- 12 pompoms, each 2cm diameter. If using double knitting yarn wrap the frame 40 times and tie 12 times.

1. Take a sheet of A4 paper, fold in half lengthways, and then in half again. Draw a diagonal line from one corner to the opposite corner and cut through all layers. This will make 3 flag shaped pieces to use as patterns.

2. Fold the strip of fabric in half lengthways and pin the pattern pieces onto the fabric. These will tesselate so very little fabric is wasted. Continue cutting the flag shapes re-using the paper patterns. Repeat with the backing fabric.

3. Placing right sides together, stitch the front and back of the flags together with a 5mm seam allowance. Trim the excess fabric from the point of the flag to reduce the bulk, before turning inside-out and pressing.

4. Fold your chosen fabric or tape used to suspend the bunting, over the raw edges of the top of each flag and pin and stitch them evenly along the whole length. Here we have cut a strip of fabric 4cm wide and pressed the edges in to form a tape 25mm wide.

5. Attach the pompoms to the bottom of each flag by passing each tie in opposite directions through the tip of each flag, tie in a double knot to secure, and then pass both the ties back through into the pompom and cut the ends off to neaten.

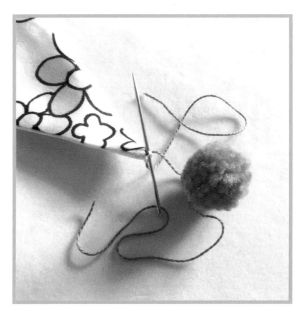

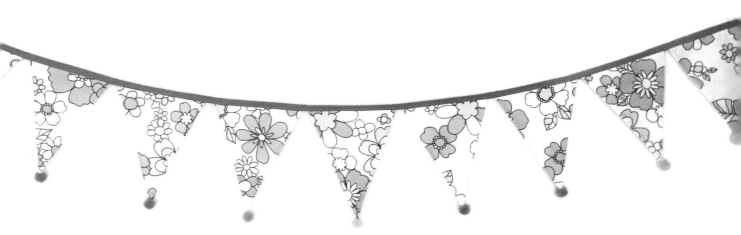

Pompom rug

Quick and easy to make using a Multipom. Nobody will be able to resist feeling it!

MATERIALS for a 60cm diameter rug:
- 60cm of 150 cm wide heavyweight calico
- 800g of double knitting acrylic yarn in colours of your choice.

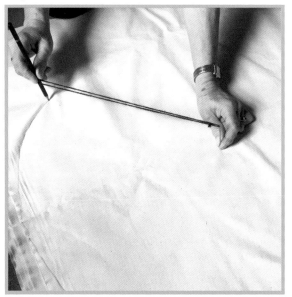

1. Fold the calico in half and cut 2 circles, each 64cm diameter. To do this, draw a circle on the fabric by threading a yarn through a needle and tie the ends together to make a loop 32cm long. Push the point of the needle into the fabric. Hold tightly in position with a pencil in the loop and keeping the thread taut, draw a circle on the fabric.

2. Continue to mark 4 more circles in the top piece of calico by positioning the needle in the same position but tying knots in the yarn to shorten it by 4cm each time. The circles will be 4cm apart.

3. Cut around the outer circle through both layers of calico. The plain circle will become the backing and the marked circle will be the base and guide for attaching the pompoms.

4. Make 128 pompoms each 6cm diameter. To do this, wrap the frame lengthways 130 times and tie 4 times. A shortcut to reduce the wrapping time is to wrap 2 strands together. Do this by either using 2 balls of the same colour, or take the end of the yarn from the centre of the ball and wrap with the end from the outside of the ball.

5. Now you are ready to start attaching the pompoms to the base fabric. To ensure the rug is perfectly round, start from the outer line, attach 36 pompoms alternating and arranging the colours. Pass the ties of each pompom through to the back of the base fabric along the line, a short distance apart from each other and tie on the back, initially with a single knot. This can be untied easily if you need to rearrange the colours or adjust them.

6. Attach the next pompom approximately 5cms further along the line and continue until 36 pompoms are evenly spaced along the outer line.

7. Working towards the centre, attach 30 pompoms to the second line, 24 to the third line and 18 to the fourth line. Fill in the centre with the remaining 20 pompoms.

8. When you are happy with the spacing and the arrangement of colours, tighten the first knot of each pompom and secure it by adding a second knot on top. Trim to neaten.

9. To assemble the rug, snip 1.5cm into the base fabric at regular intervals all around the edge.

10. Turn under a 2cm hem, pin and tack ensuring the edge forms an even curve.

11. Prepare the backing fabric as above, but snip 2cm into the edge at regular intervals and pin and tack a 2.5cm hem. The backing fabric will be very slightly smaller than the base fabric.

12. Place the backing fabric over the base fabric, wrong sides together and slip-stitch into place. To strengthen the seam, slip-stitch around the edge twice. Unpick the tacking stitches.

13. One finished rug!

NOTE:

This rug is not hard-wearing and mainly decorative, but it does look beautiful and everyone will want to feel it! Oh, and a word of warning, cats will love it!

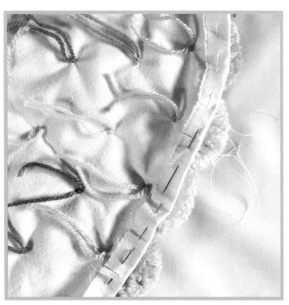

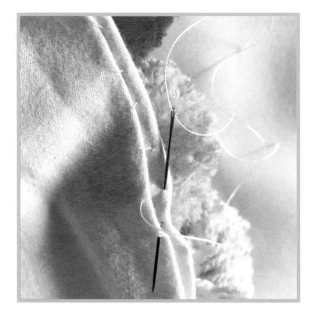

Coathanger

This coathanger is too nice to hide away in a cupboard!
It would make a gorgeous gift and is made using just 2 crochet stitches.

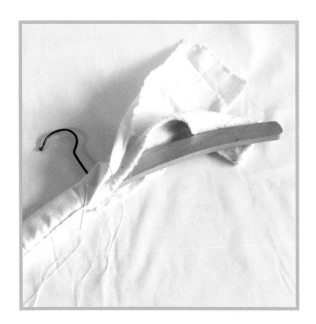

MATERIALS:
- 44cm long wooden coathanger.
- A strip of wadding 7cm x 44cm. You could use curtain interlining (bump) or a piece of blanket.
- A strip of fabric (calico or firm cotton) 10cm x 48cm.
- 5mm crochet hook.
- 50g double knitting yarn.
- 15 pompoms each 2cm diameter.

1. Using a large needle, bradawl or points of scissors, carefully push the hook of the coathanger through the centre of the wadding. Fold it over the coathanger and lace the seams together along the lower edge and around both ends.

2. Press under a 1.5 cm seam around the fabric strip and by the same method as above, push the hook through the fabric. Fold it over the wadding and stitch it tightly along the lower edge and around both ends, so the coathanger is neatly covered.

3. Cast on 55ch, *1dc, 1dc into each ch to end* Repeat this for another 12 rows.

4. Pass the centre of the crocheted strip over the coathanger hook. Join the two sides together along the lower edge with 1dc into each stitch. Slip stitch both ends together.

5. Make 10 pompoms by wrapping the frame lengthways 40 times and tying 10 times. Make an additional 5 pompoms by wrapping the frame widthways 40 times and tying 5 times.

6. Attach the 15 pompoms along the lower edge of the coathanger using the 2 ties, knotting them and finally passing the ties back through into the pompom to conceal the ends, before cutting off.

Wreath

Experiment with colours to create an everlasting wreath, in any style and for any occasion.

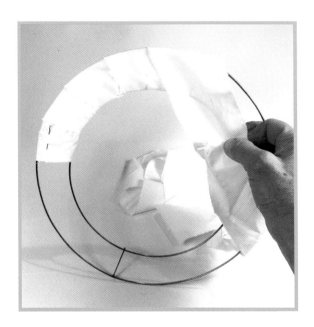

MATERIALS:
- A 25cm diameter wire florists wreath.
- A strip of fabric approximately 2m x 5cm. This could be torn from an old sheet, or any fabric pieces joined together to form a strip.
- Approximately 200g - 300g of assorted yarns.

1. Wrap the strip of fabric around the wire frame overlapping it to cover the frame completely. Stitch the ends to secure in place.

2. Make approximately 48 x 4cm diameter pompoms. These can be made 6 at a time. If using double knitting yarn, wrap the frame 80 times and tie 6 times. Attach these to the wreath by stitching them to the fabric which covers the frame (see page 8) Knot the ties of each pompom together on the back to secure. Pass them both together back through into the pompom, and trim. This will ensure the back of the wreath is neat.

3. Continue attaching the pompoms until the whole wreath is covered. Attach a loop onto the back of the wreath to hang it. A ribbon bow or smaller pompoms can be added in contrasting colours.

Door curtain

A colourful decoration for your home.
A door curtain made using pompoms of different sizes and drinking straws!

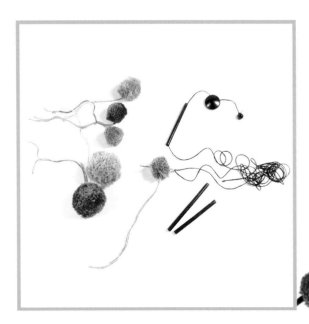

MATERIALS for a 50cm wide curtain:
- 3 x 100g balls of double knitting cotton in colours of your choice.
- Drinking straws - we've used black plastic ones cut into approximately 7cm lengths.
- 1m tape 2.5cm wide.
- A rod to fit the width of your door.
- Round beads for the bottom of the strings.
- Strong thin thread such as linen or a crochet cotton.

1. Make pompoms by wrapping the frame lengthways:
   120 times and tie 5 times
   90 times and tie 6 times
   75 times and tie 8 times
   50 times and tie 11 times
with each of 3 colours to make 90 pompoms.

2. Cut the strong thread the height of the door frame plus 20 cm. Pass one end through the bead and knot the thread around the bead to secure. Add another bead for extra weight if required.

3. Using a sharp needle, thread a length of drinking straw onto the thread.

4. Next, carefully thread a pompom onto the string, ensuring the thread passes through the centre of the pompom. Follow with another drinking straw and continue to alternate until the length of thread is full.

5. Repeat until you have enough strings to fill the width of your door

6. Stitch each string equidistantly on to the tape, and then wrap and lace it around the rod. This will ensure your door curtain is strong and rigid at the top and can be secured into place.

Knitted teacosy

An easy pattern for the beginner knitters out there.

MATERIALS for a 17cm tall teapot:
- 100g double knitting yarn.
- 5mm knitting needles.
- Oddments of different coloured yarns for the pompoms. We've used 60 pompoms, in 6 different rainbow colours, 10 of each colour.

1. Cast on 52 stitches.

2. K2, P2 for 15cms

3. K1, (K2 tog) to end of row (39sts)

4. K1, P2 to end

5. K1, K2tog to last 2 sts, K2tog (26 sts)

6. P to end

7. K2 tog to last st, K1 (7sts)

8. Pass yarn through the remaining 7 sts, draw together and fasten off.

9. Repeat the above to make the other side of the teacosy.

10. Pin and stitch both sides together leaving an opening for the spout and the handle.

11. Make the small pompoms. If using double knitting, wrap the frame 40 times and tie 12 times. Repeat with each colour. Wet the pompoms to make extra fluffy and trim them to make them dense.

12. Arrange the pompoms evenly down the ribs of the cosy in an arrangement of your choice. Attach by passing each tie through to the back of the cosy, a short distance away from each other. Tie securely in a knot, pass them both back through the front into the pompom, before trimming off.

ALTERNATIVES:
- Either add a large pompom to the top of the teacosy or lots of little ones.
- Decorate a ready made teacosy or coffee pot cover.

Fabric shoulder bag

Make this bag in any size, style, using any fabric and either hand or machine stitch it.

MATERIALS for a 30cm wide bag:
- 1/4m of 115cm or 160cm wide fabric for the outside of the bag.
- 1/4m of 115cm or 160cm wide fabric for the lining.
- 1m 2.5cm wide cotton tape or a co-ordinating cord for the strap.
- Yarn for the pompoms to co-ordinate with the fabric.
- A button or toggle (optional).

1. Make a pattern by placing a round plate or tray onto a piece of paper (we used a 32cm diameter plate). Draw halfway around it and then continue the line outwards at an angle for another 8cms. Draw a line across the top.

2. Double the fabrics if possible, and pin the pattern onto them to cut 2 pieces each of fabric and lining.

3. If making a strap, cut a strip of fabric 8cm wide and the length you require (about 80 cm should be sufficient for a shoulder bag). If your fabric isn't wide enough, join it in the middle.

4. Press a 1cm seam along the length of strap. Place the cotton tape on the wrong side of the fabric, fold over the raw edge and fold the pressed edge over the top of it. Slip stitch or machine stitch down the middle of the strap along the folded seam.

5. Placing right sides together stitch a 1cm seam around the curved edges of the fabric. Clip the curves in the seam allowance, turn the fabric out the right way and press. Repeat with the lining, but don't turn it inside out. Press a 1cm seam allowance along both top edges, put the lining into the bag and pin together.

6. Insert the ends of the strap (or cord) into each side of the bag, between the lining and the outer fabric. Pin it in place.

7. If required, insert a loop along the middle of one side, long enough to fold over to the other side around a pompom, button or toggle, to fasten the bag. Pin in place.

8. Top-stitch or slip-stitch around the top of the bag ensuring the strap or cord and the loop, if used, are both very securely attached into the seam.

9. Make a 1cm pleat on both the front and back of the bag along the top edge by pulling all layers of fabric together with a securing stitch. Incorporate the loop within one of the pleats.

10. Make pompoms in the size and colour of your choice. Here 4 colours have been wrapped together selecting yarns to match the colours in the fabric. The predominant colour of pink was wrapped more times than the other colours. 8 pompoms were made, 4 at a time, each 6cm diameter. These were attached along the top of the bag. Attach a button to fasten the bag together with the loop.

ALTERNATIVES:
- This project could be sewn by hand.
- Consider upcycling fabric. This bag has been made from a 'not to be worn again' skirt, using the coordinating lining of the skirt to line the bag.
- Add pompoms to a ready-made bag.

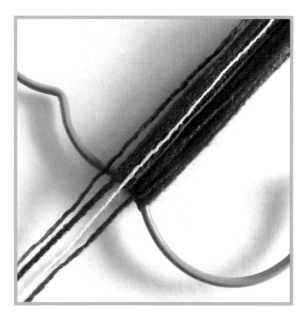

45

Knitted scarf

With simple knitting skills create this exquisite soft, cosy and unique pompom scarf.
A great accessory for any outfit.

MATERIALS:
- 2 x 50g balls of Sirdar Click double knitting yarn.
- Size 5 knitting needles.

To knit the scarf:
- Cast on 1 st
- Row 1. (increasing) K1 into back of st (2sts)
- Row 2. P
- Repeat rows 1 & 2 until 50 sts are on needle
- Continue K1 row, P1 row for 50cms
- K2 tog (decreasing), K rest of row (49sts)
- P next row
- Continue until 1st remains and fasten off

Make pompoms in varying sizes:
- Wrap the frame widthways 150 times and tie 2 times
- Wrap the frame lengthways 125 times and tie 5 times
- Wrap the frame lengthways 100 times and tie 6 times
- Wrap the frame lengthways 90 times and tie 7 times
- Wrap the frame widthways 80 times and tie 4 times
- Wrap the frame widthways 50 times and tie 5 times
- Wrap the frame widthways 35 times and tie 6 times
- Wrap the frame widthways 30 times and tie 8 times

Attaching:
Using the ties, attach the pompoms to the curved edge
of the scarf, with the largest ones at each end, decreasing
in size towards the middle. Pass the ends back through
into the pompoms and cut off.

Handwarmers & hat

Using super chunky yarn will make fast work of this snuggly knitted hat and matching handwarmers. It uses just 2 stitches, so ideal for a novice knitter.

Materials:
- 3 X 50g balls of Sirdar Big Softie Super Chunky yarn
- a small amount of matching thin but strong yarn to tie the pompoms.
- Size 1 (7.5mm) knitting needles.

1. To knit the handwarmers:
- Cast on 20sts leaving a long end to sew together.
- K1 row, P 1 row (6 times) for rib.
- P 1 row, K 1 row for 13cm, ending with a P row.
- Cast off, leaving a long end to sew together.
- Sew side seams, leaving a gap for the thumb.

2. To knit the hat:
- Cast on 50 sts leaving a long end to stitch togather.
- K 1 row, P 1 row (6 times) for rib.
- K4, K2 tog, (K6,K2 tog) 5 times, K4 (44 sts)
- P 1 row.
- K3, K2 tog (K5, K2tog) 5 times, K4 (38 sts)
- P 1 row.
- K3, K2 tog (K4, K2 tog) 5 times, K3 (32 sts)
- P 1 row.
- K2, K 2 tog (K3, K2 tog) 5 times, K3 (26 sts)
- P 1 row.
- K2, K2tog (K2, K2tog) 5 times, K2 (20 sts)
- P 1 row.
- (K1, K2 tog) 6 times, K2 (14 sts)
- P 1 row.
- Pass end of yarn through remaining stitches, pull tight and fasten off.

3. To make 15 pompoms:
- Wrap the frame lengthways 20 times and tie 6 times. Repeat twice to make 12 pompoms each 4cm diameter.
- Wrap the frame widthways 20 times and wrap 3 times to make 3 pompoms, each 4cm diameter.
- Attach 10 pompoms around the rib of the hat.
- Plait the ties of 3 pompoms together and attach to the top of the hat.
- Attach 2 pompoms to the top of each handwarmer.

Necklace & earrings

Mix colours, textures, beads and cords to make eye-catching and unique jewellery to coordinate with an outfit.

MATERIALS:
- A selection of beads with holes large enough to thread the pompom ties through. We've used 10mm flat disc beads and 15mm round beads.
- Chunky wool in a colour of your choice - an oddment would be enough. We used just 10g to make these.
- Thinner matching thread to tie the pompoms, such as perle cotton or embroidery thread.
- 2 earwire hooks.

1. Using the chunky yarn make a cord approximately 70cm long, following the instructions on page 11.

2. Make 9 pompoms, each 2cm diameter by wrapping the frame lengthways with the chunky yarn 30 times and tying 9 times with the thinner yarn. Trim them so they are very dense.

3. Pass both the ties of the pompom firstly through the round bead, then the flat bead. Thread a needle with one of the ties, and starting at the centre of the cord, pass this through the cord. Pass the other tie through the cord a short distance away from the first, and tie both together with a double knot to secure. Thread the needle with both ties and pass these back through the cord, the two beads and the pompom, then trim to neaten. If it's not possible to pass the ties back through the beads, secure them within the cord.

4. Continue attaching the beads and pompoms evenly along the cord until you have 7 in position.

5. Tie the cord neatly at both ends.

6. Make the matching earrings by passing the ties through the beads as above and securing them by tying together through the loop at the base of the ear wire.

ALTERNATIVES:
- Any amount and combination of beads can be used.
- Upcycle old jewellery, using both the beads and findings.
- Attach fastenings to the ends of the cord if preferred, using jewellery findings.

Hair, bag & shoe accessories

Get together with friends and have fun making some colourful accessories.

MATERIALS:
- a selection of hair elastics, hairslides, hairbands, brooch backs, shoe clips, keyrings or anything else you wish to decorate.

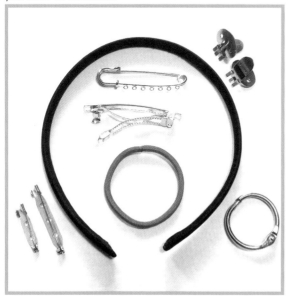

1. Make a selection of pompoms in colours of your choice using small oddments of double knitting yarn. Here we have made 25 pompoms each 2cm diameter in 5 different colours. Wrap the frame widthways 40 times and tie 5 times. Use a 40cm length of yarn to tie them and make sure these ties are not cut off, as they will be used to attach.

2. Attach the pompoms to the hair elastics by tying, using the ties with which the pompoms were made. The ends can be passed back through into the pompom.

3. The pompoms can be attached to the brooches, hairslides and shoe clips by passing the ties through the holes or around the bars and tying to secure.

4. For the bag charm or keyring tie 3 pompoms together with the ties, as near as possible to the pompoms. Take each pair of colour ties and plait them together. Attach the ties to the keyring with a secure knot.

5. Decorate the hairband by either tying the pompoms to it, or if preferred, use a fabric covered one and stitch the pompoms onto it, passing the ends back into the pompoms. Additionallly, ribbons or other trimmings could be added between the pompoms.

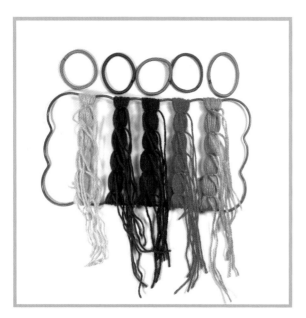

Patriotic poms

Use this method to pompom a flag, design or picture of your choice.

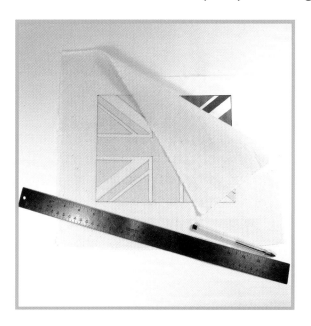

MATERIALS:
- an image of your choice printed onto paper.
- a piece of firm cotton or calico, larger than your image.
- oddments of double knitting yarn.
- a thin but strong yarn to tie the pompoms.
- a firm piece of card the same size as your image.

1. Copy and print a colour image of a flag, the size of your choice onto an A4 sheet of paper. Ours is 16cm x 25cm.

2. Take a rectangle of firm calico or heavy cotton about 8cm larger all round than the image and trace it onto the fabric. If you can't see the image through the fabric, hold it up to a window, so the light shines through it.

3. To make the pompoms we used double knitting yarn and tied the pompoms with an embroidery cotton. The number will vary according to the size of the image but we used the following:

RED - 20 x 2.5cm diameter by wrapping the frame lengthways 50 times and tying 10 times; repeat twice.
RED - 32 x 1.5cm diameter by wrapping the frame lengthways 20 times and tying 16 times; repeat twice.
BLUE - 24 x 2cm diameter by wrapping the frame lengthways 40 times and tying 12 times; repeat twice.
BLUE - 40 x 1.5cm diameter by wrapping the frame lengthways 20 times and tying 16 times; repeat twice. Additionally wrap the frame widthways 20 times and tie 8 times.
WHITE - 28 x 1.5cm diameter by wrapping the frame lengthways 20 times and tying 16 times; repeat twice.
WHITE - 72 x 1cm diameter by wrapping the frame lengthways 15 times and tying 18 times, repeat 4 times.

4. Using the paper copy as a guide, attach the pompoms to the fabric, following the instructions on page 8, ensuring they are close together and touching each other.

5. When the image is totally covered, cut a piece of firm card, the same size as the flag. Fold the side edges of the calico over the card to the back and using a strong thread lace them tightly together. Repeat with the top and bottom edges. This will give a neat finish so the flag can be displayed by hanging or framing.

Cheeky chicks

Half a dozen little chicks in an egg box!

MATERIALS:
- 25g yellow double knitting yarn.
- Six 40cm lengths of darker yellow or orange double knitting yarn (for the chicks legs)
- A 10cm square (or scraps) of orange felt.
- 12 self-adhesive goggly eyes.
- An empty egg box.

1. Using the yellow yarn make 6 pompoms, each 4cm diameter by wrapping the frame lengthways 80 times. Make 6 ties using the 40cm lengths of darker yellow or orange yarn (the chicks legs)

2. Cut 18 pieces of orange felt, each 2cm square. These will become 6 beaks and 12 feet.

3. Taking 12 of the squares, cut little curves from each of the 4 sides to make their feet.

4. Tie 2 knots in each leg. The first one about 4cm down from the body (knees) and another 4cm lower (ankles)

5. Thread the end of each leg through a needle and pass this through the centre of each foot. Tie another knot underneath each foot to stop it dropping off and trim to neaten.

6. For the beak, fold each square in half diagonally and place in position within the pompom. The beak can either be stitched or glued into place.

7. Attach the self-adhesive goggly eyes.

8. Repeat with the other five pompoms to make half a dozen little chicks to live in the egg box!

Angels
These adorable little angels will grace any room.

MATERIALS for 8 angels:
- An assortment of yarns, fine fabrics and nets, plain, fluffy and sparkly.
- Strong but thinish yarn for the ties.
- A thicker yarn for the legs.
- Eight 2cm diameter wooden beads and 16 smaller ones for the feet.
- Marker pens to draw the angels faces.
- Glitter pipe cleaners for the halos.
- Card for the wings.

1. Tear or cut the fabrics into 1cm wide strips, in as long lengths as possible.

2. Randomly wrap the frame with an assortment of yarns and fabrics, so it looks like the example here. It's not necessary to join the strips of fabric or yarn, just overlap them. These pompoms will be very 'thin' to make wispy skirts. Using the thinner thread, make just 2 ties along the bundle: 6cm from each end, and 12cm apart. Wrap another bundle to match the first next to it.

3. Turn the frame over and make another tie over the top of the securing ties, using the thicker yarn. These ties will form the legs.

4. Cut the pompoms off the frame and arrange the ties so the thinner ones come out of the top and the legs hang through the 'skirt'. Repeat to make another 4 pompom skirts.

5. Draw faces and hair on the beads, keeping the holes of the beads positioned top and bottom.

6. Tracing the pattern below, cut out 8 wings from the card. The pattern can be folded in half and cut on a fold to ensure the wings are symmetrical.

7. Make the halos by cutting 7cm lengths of pipe cleaner and wrapping them round a pen to form a halo shape.

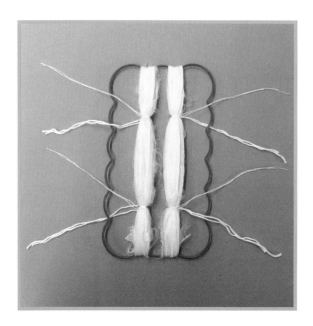

Assembling the angels

8. Pass the thinner ties either side of the centre of the wings and tie around at the front. Then pass the same ties through the angels head bead and finally through the halo. Tie securely arranging the wings and if necessary, glue the halo into place. The ties can be used to suspend the fairy.

9. For each leg, tie a knot in the thicker yarn, to form the ankles. Thread a bead onto the bottom and tie another knot below this to secure it. Trim the ends to neaten.

10. Make a cord 1.5m long following the instructions on page 11. Position the angels at approximately 15cm intervals along the cord and secure them with a knot around the cord. Neaten the ends within the cord and trim.

ALTERNATIVES:
- The angels could be hung individually
- Omit the wings and make a string of colourful dollies or ballerinas.

Holly decoration

This holly spray can be used for a variety of festive decorations.

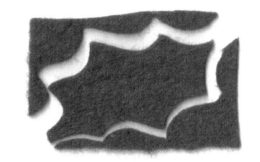

MATERIALS for each holly spray
- green felt (6cm x 10cm)
- a small amount of red yarn for the berries.
- a thin strong red yarn to tie the pompoms .

1. Cut some rectangles of green felt approximately 5cm x 3cm (two or three are required for each holly spray) Starting at one corner, cut towards the opposite corner to create holly shaped leaves. It doesn't matter if they are slightly different shapes but if you prefer, make a pattern by tracing this one.

2. Make some 1.5cm diameter red pompoms. Two or three berries are required for each spray. If using double knitting yarn, wrap the frame lengthways 20 times and tie 16 times, or if you don't need as many berries, wrap the frame widthways 20 times and tie 8 times. Use a strong but thin yarn to tie the pompoms.

3. Overlap 2 or 3 leaves at their base and attach a pompom by passing each tie through to the back of all the leaves and tying securely. Repeat with the second pompom. The ends can be passed back through into each pompom and cut off within it. Alternatively they can be left on and used to attach the holly spray to whatever you wish.

Christmas puddings

Good enough to eat pompom puddings!

MATERIALS for 4 puddings

- 25g dark brown double knitting yarn.
- A small amount of 'sultana' coloured yarn (a paler gingery brown)
- 10g soft white yarn (we've used a lightly twisted wool)
- A small square of green felt for the holly leaves.
- A small amount of red wool for the berries.
- Thin strong yarn to tie the pompoms and hang the puddings.

1. Wrap the frame 10 times with the dark brown yarn, then wrap once with the lighter brown. Repeat this 13 times, so the frame has 130 wraps of dark brown yarn and 13 wraps of the paler brown.

2. Wrap the soft white yarn around the frame on just one side. The amount of times you wrap will depend upon the thickness of yarn and how much cream you want on the top of your puddings!

3. Make 4 ties around the bundle, 6cm apart, with the end ones 3cm from each end. Gently turn the knots around so they are in the centre of the white yarn. These can then be used to suspend the puddings if required. Cut to make 4 pompoms, each 6cm diameter. Trim if necessary and make the white yarn fluffy by gently brushing with a teasel brush.

4. Make holly leaves and berries following the instructions on page 62.

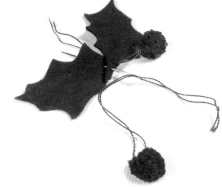

5. Taking a holly spray, and using a needle, pass each pair of ties of the red berries separately into the top of each Christmas pudding, through the pompom and tie together within the pompom using a knot to secure. Cut the ends off within the pudding.

6. The ties which were used to make the pompoms can be used to suspend the puddings if required.

Jolly robins

A cheerful little flock of robins for your home at Christmas.

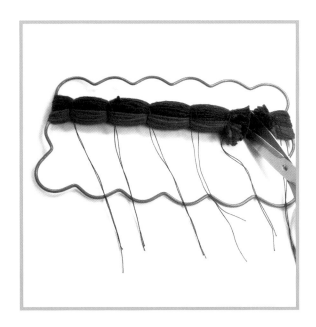

MATERIALS for 6 robins:
- 25g of brown double knitting yarn
- Approximately 5g of red double knitting yarn
- Thin strong yarn for the ties
- A small scrap of yellow felt
- 12 self adhesive goggly eyes

1. Wrap the frame lengthways 70 times using the brown yarn. Using the red yarn, continue to wrap to one side of the brown bundle another 10 times. Tie 6 times, using the thin strong yarn, to make six pompoms each 4cm diameter.

2. Cut 6 pieces of yellow felt for the beaks, each approximately 1cm square. Attach them to the pompoms, between the brown body and the red breast, by the same method as the chicks on page 58.

3. Position the goggly eyes above the beak.

4. Use the thread of the ties to hang up if required.